POLAR BEARS:

An Illustrated Book for Kids 4-8

+65 Breathtaking Facts and HD Photos That Will Amaze Children and Their Adults!

CIEL PUBLISHING

© **Copyright 2018 - All rights reserved.**

The contents of this book may not be reproduced, duplicated or transmitted without direct written permission from the author.

Under no circumstances will any legal responsibility or blame be held against the publisher for any reparation, damages, or monetary loss due to the information herein, either directly or indirectly.

Legal Notice:
You cannot amend, distribute, sell, use, quote or paraphrase any part of the content within this book without the consent of the author.

Disclaimer Notice:
Please note the information contained within this document is for educational and entertainment purposes only. No warranties of any kind are expressed or implied. Readers acknowledge that the author is not engaging in the rendering of legal, financial, medical or professional advice.

By reading this document, the reader agrees that under no circumstances is the author responsible for any losses, direct or indirect, which are incurred as a result of the use of information contained within this document, including, but not limited to, ―errors, omissions, or inaccuracies.

Thank You for Purchasing This Book!

In this small book you will find amazing facts (that defy logic) about a very small but mysterious animal: bats!

Hopefully, with the information provided you will further understand these creatures and how great they are.

I hope you're ready for the journey ahead!

Fact #1

Polar bears have one of the best senses of smell on the planet. In fact, their senses are so enhanced, they can smell their prey even at a distance of 10 to 15 kilometers away!

Fact #2

A polar bear's layer of fat is known as their "blubber" which, along with a thick layer of fur on their body, guards them against their very cold environments. These guys sure know how to keep warm!

Fact #3

They may appear white on the outside, but they're really black on the inside. Polar bears have a third layer that protects them against the cold and it's their black skin underneath everything. Dark skin helps absorb the sun's rays and keeps them warm in daylight.

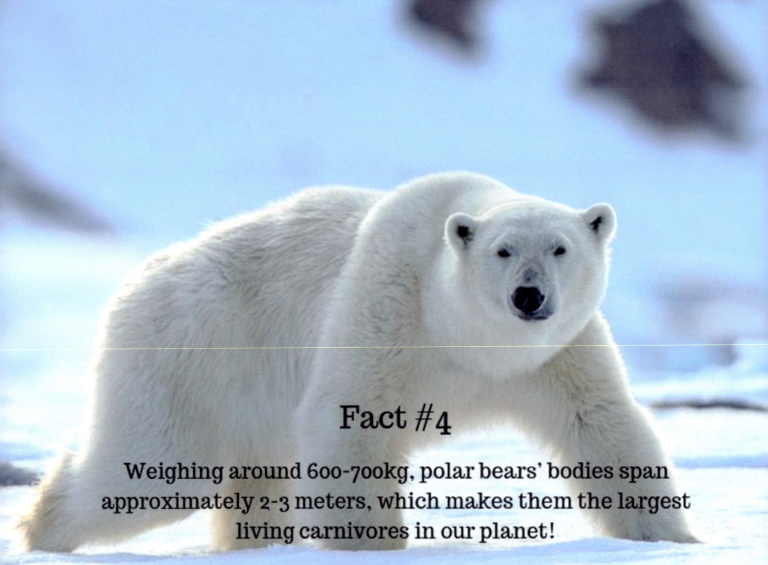

Fact #4

Weighing around 600-700kg, polar bears' bodies span approximately 2-3 meters, which makes them the largest living carnivores in our planet!

Fact #5

Misconceived as land animals, polar bears are some of the best swimmers around and can even drift 100 kilometers offshore and make it back home. Whoever said bears can't swim?

Fact #6

Webbed paws, sometimes as big and long as one foot, enable the polar bears to swim at high speeds of 10km/h and keep themselves steady in the water.

Fact #7

Polar bears are very intelligent, and they use their smarts to make up for what they lack in movement, agility, and speed on land. If these guys took tests, I'm pretty sure they would ace them!

Fact #8

Contrary to popular belief, a polar bear's fur isn't white!
If you observe the colors properly, you'll find
it's transparent/translucent - a trait that allows polar bears
to easily camouflage or blend into their environments

Fact #9

At birth, polar bear cubs are the size of guinea pigs (25-40cm)
and sometimes even smaller! How cute!

Fact #10

Speaking of birth, did you know that female polar bears go into
special snow dens to give birth to their offspring
in the months of November and December?

Fact #11

The whole family moves into these dens to cater to the needs of mama bear giving birth and, after the procedure has finished, everyone moves out within four to five months.

Fact #12

In polar bear circles, raising the cub automatically becomes the responsibility of the mother. Cubs stay with their mom for around two years so they can learn how to survive their harsh habitat.

Fact #13

Polar bears can be found in the colder regions of Canada, Alaska, Greenland, Russia, Norway, and, last but not least, Antarctica!

Fact #14

Sadly, polar bears are facing the consequences of climate change and their habitats are slowly melting away because of increasing temperatures around the globe. Soon, they may no longer have a place to call home!

Fact #15

Due to their natural tendencies to spend all their time on ice and on the sea, polar bears belong to a special subcategory of mammals called "marine mammals".

Fact #16

You already know that polar bears can swim fast and for long distances, but did you know that they're also able to swim for days and days on end without having to leave the water? I wish I could do that!

Fact #17

If you sit down and add up all the math behind polar bears' hunting trips, you'd come to the finding that more than half their life is spent hunting!

Fact #18

Despite all this hunting, only around 2-3% of a polar bear's lifetime hunts are successful. These guys are persistent!

Fact #19

A new breakthrough in today's world is that WWF, after having worked with firm SPYGEN, can now extract a polar bear's DNA from just their footprint in the snow!

Fact #20

This DNA reveals a lot of information about that certain polar and it is isolated from not only the footprint but also from some seal that the polar bear recently devoured.

Fact #21

Aside from climate change, polar bears are having their home taken away by humans looking to expand their oil and gas operations. Hopefully, they will stop before it's too late!

Fact #22

Oil spills on the sea surface greatly diminish the insulating effect of a bear's fur. Now, these poor bears have to work harder and eat more just to keep warm.

Fact #23

Another devastating effect of an oil spill is that polar bears can be poisoned if they are too close to the spill. Often, this can cause their death.

Fact #24

Did you know that if you combine polar bears and grizzly bears you get "Grolar" bears and "Pizzly" bears? These animals are called hybrids and first one of its kind was found in 2006.

Fact #25

Although grolar and pizzly bears are a mix of two bear species, they behave and act more like traditional polar bears. They stomp, hurl and lay down just like regular polar bears do!

Fact #26

Did you know that 150,000 years ago, grizzly and polar bears were one in the same? Although they drifted genetically, they're still like long-lost cousins.

Fact #27

According to studies done by the WWF (World Wildlife Fund), there are only around 30,000 polar bears in the entire planet. That's around the size of the town you live in.

Fact #28

WWF also predicts that by the year 2050, the total population of polar bears from around the world would have declined by 30% (or 10,000) because of climate change.

Fact #29

Fun fact! Did you know you can actually adopt a polar bear from the WWF website? Although it's unlikely you'll ever take one home, it's nice gesture that will likely save many bears' life.

Fact #30

Aside from eating grubs like ringed and bearded seals, which almost counts as their exclusive diet, polar bears have been seen eating walruses, whale carcasses, and even bird eggs.

Fact #31

Mother polar bears are only able to give birth up to 5 times in their life and, because of this, they are amongst the mammals with the lowest rates of reproduction.

Fact #32

Coupled with their incredulous layers of skin, abilities, and intelligence for hunting, polar bears walk around with a full set of 42 teeth in their mouth! Ouch!

Fact #33

Did you know that the scientific name of these amazing animals is "Ursus maritimus"? A very serious-sounding name to such a cute animal indeed!

Fact #34

Aside from "Ursus maritimus", polar bears are also known by the following names: Thalarctos, sea bear, ice bear, Nanuq, isbjorn, white bear, beliy medved, lord of the Arctic, old man in the fur cloak, and white sea deer.

Fact #35

Want to know how fast they go? Well, these guys can reach speeds of 40km/h on land and 10km/h in the water. Yup, they can be faster than us humans!

Fact #36

Polar bears move around a lot, with their travels depending on the quality of ice present in their region and if there's any grubs, seals, and other prey to eat around the area.

Fact #37

Scientists have found that polar bears are only expected to survive a time of 220 days (their fasting period) in an ice-region where there is a lack of suitable prey available for them to eat. This is just enough for them to hibernate during the winter.

Fact #38

On days where the weather is extremely cold and windy, polar bears dig holes/pits for shelters. Then, they curl up in balls and cover up their muzzle with their paws to protect it from the wind. I'm sure you've done it too, even if you're a polar bear!

Fact #39

Even though they live in the coldest conditions on Earth, polar bears tend to overheat when they run due to overexertion. This doesn't happen when they walk since their pace is casual and restful.

Fact #40

Global climate is constantly changing and as a result, so does the shape and structure of ice habitats. Due to this lack of a fixed region, polar bears don't mark their own habitat like other mammals but just travel around as they deem fit.

Fact #41

Polar bears tend to travel under 1000 km to set up homes but scientists used a satellite to track a female bear who trekked for around 5000km, from Alaska to Canada to Greenland!

Fact #42

From the 19 polar regions in the world and out of approximately 25000 polar bears present around the world, 60% of them have made their home in regions of Canada.

Fact #43

A Norwegian scientist, Nils Oristlands showed that polar bears consume twice the energy as compared to other mammals and they overheat because of increased consumption of oxygen and more absorption of heat.

Fact #44

His studies also went on to show how polar bears who are in a state of running use 13 times the energy used by polar bears who are walking over the same distance.

Fact #45

In the Spring, as the ice starts to melt, adult male polar bears prepare for mating and this period of mating lasts from the month of April till the month of June.

Fact #46

Polar bears don't become adults at 18 like humans. Male polar are considered mature between the ages of 6 to 10 whilst, on the other hand, female polar bears reach adulthood between ages four and six.

Fact #47

Mating between the polar bears does not occur in special dens or shelters, but rather on the sea ice. After mating, the male polar bears stay around the females for a few days before leaving to resume their everyday routine.

Fact #48

Fertile eggs don't implant in the female polar bear until the following Fall season - this process is called delayed implantation and only occurs if the mother has consumed enough fat to keep herself and the cubs healthy.

Fact #49

A polar bear's paws act like their built-in socks because of the way they're covered with fur at the bottom. This helps polar bears with traction on slippery surfaces and muffles their sound as they approach their prey.

Fact #50

The only purpose of a polar bear's fat isn't to keep him/her warm. The fat also acts as a reserve of energy in cases of emergency and helps the polar bears float as they swim.

Fact #51

A polar bear's everyday routine consists of approximately 20 hours of rest and sleeping. When they're not sleeping, they're out looking for prey, which they eat every 4 to 5 days!

Fact #52

Popular folklores and pop culture would have you believe that polar bears hibernate in the winters as well, but in reality, that isn't the case. Unlike their brown and black bear counterparts, polar bears don't hibernate.

Fact #53

To deal with their issue of overheating and body temperature, polar bears love to roll around in the snow (and clean themselves in the process) and when that doesn't work, they take a dip into the ice-cold water around them.

Fact #54

Since polar bears have no natural predators, humans are the only species that threaten their existence. This, alongside scarce numbers of suitable prey available, contributes to the short lifespan of young cubs.

Fact #55

Polar bears have a special liver inside their body that enables them to store a lot of Vitamin A and as a result, they survive longer, evolve more quickly, and have an emergency supply of Vitamin A.

Fact #56

Because of the oil in their water-repellent fur, polar bears can easily shake off any water and ice that is left on their body from during their routine activities.

Fact #57

The Inuit people tend to hunt for polar bears in the wild but their activities have been strictly reduced by a quota on hunting from the Polar Bears International.

Fact #58

Inuit hunters call polar bears "nanuk" and consider them to be wise creatures that deserve to be followed and are almost man-like, giving them a near godly status.

Fact #59

Hunters also pay their homage to a polar bear by hanging the skin in an igloo for a couple of days and praying to the bear's "tatkok" (soul).

Fact #60

Sami people are scared of calling polar bears by their name in the fear of offending the animal and instead they use names like "God's dog" or "old man in the fur cloak".

Fact #61

To help the cause of polar bears and the climate change they face, WWF advocated for the creation of Polar Bear Pass National Wildlife Area in Canada, and the Russian Arctic Par in Russia.

Fact #62

Alongside this, WWF has provided extensive financial support to the Wrangel Island Nature Reserve, known as the "polar bear nursery" for its high concentration of polar bear maternity dens.

Fact #63

The most recent development for polar bears was the Polar Bear Conservation Management Plan by the US, where 115 million acres of federal waters were declared to be protected property.

Congratulations for Making It to the End!

I hope you enjoyed this journey into the lives of bats.

You now know more about bats than most human beings in the planet!

How does that feel?

Go ahead and spread your new knowledge with friends and family members.

They will be astonished!

Best-Selling Titles by the Author:

Rubik's Cube Solution Guide for Kids (3x3x3 and 2x2x2) in Full Color
http://bit.ly/Rubiks4Kids

Riddles for Kids: 365 Riddles for Daily Laughs and Giggles
http://bit.ly/RiddlesKids

First Word Search for Kids: 101 Fun with Sight Words, Early Nouns, Phonics & More!
http://bit.ly/FirstWordSearch

Inspiring Quotes for Kids: A Children's Coloring Book
http://bit.ly/InspiringQ

Dragon Coloring Book: Zen Dragons
http://bit.ly/DragonColor

Ah, I almost forgot about your FREE Gift!

If you want to get a copy of a pdf copy of **Captain Ren's Trip to Mars,** a children's book for ages 4-7, then simply scan the QR Code below and become part of our email list! You'll also get other free goodies. See you there!

And lastly… If you liked this book, please leave a review!

Amazon reviews from our readers help us keep producing quality content. We're counting with yours!

Thanks!